EMAIL MARKETI.

HOW TO GAIN SUBSCRIBERS, GROW YOUR LIST AND MAKE SALES

BY SMART READS

Free Audiobook

As a thank you for being a Smart Reader you can choose 2 FREE audiobooks from audible.com. Simply sign up for free by visiting www.audibletrial.com/Travis to get your books.

Visit:
www.smartreads.co/freebooks
to receive Smart Reads books for FREE

Check us out on Instagram:
www.instagram.com/smart_readers
@smart_readers

ABOUT SMARTREADS

Choose Smart Reads and get smart every time. Smart Reads sorts through all the best content and condenses the most helpful information into easily digestible chunks.

We design our books to be short, easy to read and highly informative. Leaving you with maximum understanding in the least amount of time.

Smart Reads aims to accelerate the spread of quality information so we've taken the copyright off everything we publish and donate our material directly to the public domain. You can read our uncopyright below.

We believe in paying it forward and donate 5% of our net sales to Pencils of Promise to build schools, train teachers and support child education.

To limit our footprint and restore forests around the globe we are planting a tree for every 10 hardcover books we sell.

Thanks for choosing Smart Reads and helping us help the planet.

Sincerely,

Travis & the Smart Reads Team

TABLE OF CONTENTS

[?]

INTRODUCTION

Email marketing is still popular than ever. Why? Because it's still the best way of building up a loyal base of customers. When social media exploded on the scene a few years ago, marketers thought email would be dead soon. Not only has it survived the storm, it's come out stronger than ever before. Essentially, if you want more sales, building an emailing list is the way to do it. But what is an email list?

Maybe you've got some contacts arranged in list-form in your Outlook or Gmail. Maybe you thought that was an emailing list. But it isn't. Not really.

When online marketers talk about email lists, they're not talking about a bunch of random contacts on their Gmail. They're taking about opt-in, professionally and legally built-up email lists where your "contacts" have actually requested that you put them there so that you can send them weekly, monthly or even daily newsletters. This is a big difference from an email list made up of work colleagues, family members, friends and ex-partners who really don't want you to get in touch with them on a daily or weekly basis.

The emailing list is a very specific type of list:

• You'll make more money from this emailing list because the people who are on there actually want to be there.

• You'll be complying with CAN-SPAM laws, which means you can rest peacefully and have the knowledge that you aren't doing anything illegal.

• You'll be building a super-useful business asset that connects you to your most promising customers who keep returning for more purchases. This results in predictable revenue, which is exactly what all startups should be aiming for .

• A proper emailing list is secure and backed-up, so that you don't have to worry about your customers' sensitive information being compromised.

An auto-responder doesn't guarantee the security of your emailing list, but it does make it easier to secure and back-up. You'll learn how to do this later on in the book. For now, let's go over some key email marketing definitions you'll easily come across.

CHAPTER 1: KEY EMAIL MARKETING DEFINITIONS

Opt-In

If you've ever written a client before, you've probably been told to include an opt-in line at the end of the text. It's a call to action (CTA) that compels a customer to do something you want them to do once they've finished reading the article. Maybe the client wants the customer to take a further look around their website, or maybe they want them to make a purchase.

What does it mean in email marketing? Opting in simply means that a person agrees to subscribe to an emailing list. They are "opting in" - as opposed to opting out.

Opt-In Form

There needs to be somewhere for the customer to opt-in, and this comes in the form of the opt-in form. It's simply a brief online web form, which customers fill in. Usually, all it requires is their email address, but some marketers ask for other information, such as their age range and location.

Opt-Out

Yep, just like there is an opt-in, there is also an opt-out. Once a customer has opted-into being on your emailing list, there is no guarantee that they're going to want to stay there. After a few weeks or months, they might decide to quit. In which case, they'll "opt-out."

Your MUST include an "unsubscribe" option with every email you send out. Otherwise, it's just bad practice and reflects poorly on your brand. Moreover, it's also compliant with the aforementioned CAN-SPAM laws, and not including one is technically illegal so it's better to have that in there. You always know when someone has opted-out because you will be given an notification.

Auto-Responder

If you want to build your own opt-in form, you need to get yourself an auto-responder. This is an essential email marketing tool that lets you build your form, expand your email list, take care of your contacts, as well as schedule your emails. It can also do a lot of other things, too.

You can go into email marketing without one of these, but it isn't recommend. An auto-responder saves you so much time that it would be crazy not to get yourself one. Some are free, but the best ones require you to pay a monthly fee. You'll find some examples later in the book.

Auto-Responder Series

An Auto-responder series are numerous emails that are emailed to your subscribers in batches. They are sent to your subscribers according to time, which is neatly based on whenever they chose to opt-into your list.

It's commonplace for a subscriber to receive an automated response almost instantly after they've opted in. Usually, your email will include a link to their freebie, as well as a welcome to your newsletter.

Squeeze Page

A squeeze page is just another name for the web page where a customer opts-into your email list. The page should host your opt-in form, and usually has nothing else. The idea is that the customer either opts-in or just heads somewhere else. You don't want to distract them with lots of other information and links as doing so will only reduce your conversion rates. Cut out any other navigation options and just focus on the opt-in form. Free from all other distractions, a customer is far likelier to opt-in.

Landing Page

Your landing page is typically the page that a site visitor should in theory see first when they enter your website. But it really depends on where they've come from or what link they've clicked on.

Ideally, your landing page is the page that lets your customers know what you're all about. It contains the right amount of information, it gets them to opt-in to your list, it gets them to make a purchase, or it gets them to fill out a form or otherwise make contact with you. In other words, a landing page gets people to do something.

You've seen landing pages many times yourself. Each time you click on a website, you're probably on a landing page. Check out some examples to get a feel for what they are, and what the best ones look like.

Conversion
This may be a term you've already heard of. Maybe you've heard clients talking about "improving conversion rates." In email marketing, it simply means when a site visitor converts from a mere visitor to an actual subscriber. When they do that, you have made a conversion.

You can track your conversion rates via analytics, which is highly recommended. If you don't, you simply won't have a clue how successful your squeeze page is, and whether or not there are things you need to do to boost your conversion rate.

Conversion Rate

Speaking of conversion rates, this is the percentage of people who have helped you to reach your conversion target.

Let's say that one-hundred people have visited your squeeze page in the last week and twenty of them have opted-into your emailing list. That gives you a conversion rate of 20%. As such, the higher your conversion rate it, the more successful you will be. Don't expect sky-high conversion rates, though.

If your conversion rate isn't 100, 90, 80 or even 70%, don't worry. Why? Because it's common for most squeeze pages to achieve an average conversion rate of somewhere in the middle of ten and fifty percent. In fact, 50% is considered very high, while 10% is still decent. It needs work, but it's a start. If, as a beginner, you manage to hit 30%, you're doing brilliant.

Again, without data you won't have a clue what your conversion rate is. Download an analytics tool to help you keep track of these things.

Deliverability Rate

This is the percentage of your email subscribers who are receiving emails from your auto-responder. You might think this sounds a bit puzzling - after all, shouldn't the deliverability rate be 100%? Ideally, yes. And it usually is. But if it's 99% or less, it usually means there is an incorrect email address in your mailing list. Root out the bad email addresses and then continue.

Sometimes, however, the number is 99% or lower because an email address has used a spam filter to block your email.

Also, it's probably not worth mentioning as you're likely already figured it out but just because a person has received an email it doesn't mean they have opened it. Deliverability rate just shows you how many emails have been delivered.

Open Rate

Your open rate refers to the percentage of your subscribers who have opened an email you sent out. Deliverability rate lets you know how many received it, while open rate tells you how many took action and opened it. The average is 25%. If you can match that or even beat it, you're doing well.

Analytics

Analytics in this sense is a tool that collects data from your website and lets you know how well your website is doing. It tells you things such as how many visitors you've had over a certain period, how long people stayed on the pages, what actions they took, and so on.

It's a key tool in email marketing as it lets you know what you're doing right with your website and what you're doing wrong. For example, if your squeeze page is getting plenty of visitors but hardly any conversions, this tells you that you need to tweak it.

Similarly if people are visiting your landing page but leaving after just a second or so, it tells you that your landing page needs a lot of work. See, page views only tell you that you're doing a good job of driving traffic to your site. But they don't tell you how much enjoyment or value a visitor is getting out of your page. Having 500 page views in 24 hours might sound amazing, but if they all leave your page after just two seconds, what use is that?

At this stage, you need an analytics tool that tells you how many page views you're getting on your squeeze page and what your conversion rate is.

CHAPTER 2: GETTING INSIDE AN EMAIL SUBSCRIBER'S MINDSET

To really know what kind of emails you should be sending out to your subscribers, you need to first of all understand their mindset. Now, getting into someone's mind and probing around for clues as to what their motivations are isn't easy, and this is why there's analytics to the rescue.

But you know what subscribers REALLY want from you? Free stuff! This might irk you to hear it at first. "Gosh darn freeloaders," you might mutter. But why shouldn't people want free stuff from you? A lot of the world's top entrepreneurs are giving away stuff for free ALL THE TIME.

In fact, you may have noticed on social media how the people you follow seem to be giving away stuff for free all the time. There is one entrepreneur in particular who is well-known for giving away expensive luxury cars for free pretty much all the time. "How can they afford to do that?" you might be asking. "Won't they be broke?"

No way! They know the importance and value of giving stuff away for free. It helps you get more fans and subscribers who you can then sell the really premium stuff to at a later date.

So who cares if people want free stuff from you all the time? Give them what they want! They will become customers who will go on to buy stuff from you eventually.

So what kind of stuff can you give away for free?

1.) A report – This doesn't have to be long. Just a few pages on a certain topic will do. Reports are always super useful and people love them.

2.) A cheat sheet - This is an awesome thing to give away for free. People love cheat sheets. Give them one for free and they'll love you forever.

3.) An educational video - Because people will always prefer to watch rather than read

4.) An audio file - And if they're not watching, they're listening instead

5) A webinar - Webinars are super popular right now. If you're hosting one soon, now is your chance to get people on board with your brand and message by inviting them for free. Your webinar should offer them

valuable information, and you could also use it to promote a product.

But What Do Your Subscribers Truly Want?
To fully understand your subscribers' mindset, you need to divide your subscribers into two types:

1.) Fans
2.) Solution Seekers

Your fans are your loyal followers who have probably been following you on social media for a while now. They know you and want to stay connected. They're not really after something in particular from you; it's more that they just want to retain that sense of connection.

However, despite them not wanting anything particular, fans prove their worth by purchasing pretty much everything you have to offer. They want to support you in any way they can, and they'll buy and share your stuff. But what if you've got fans who aren't yet on your email list? Go and ask them to sign up! What are you waiting for?

Solution seekers are a bit different from your fans. They have a specific problem, and they hope that you've got the solution.

You as a reader might also be a solution seeker yourself. Perhaps you've got a problem that you're hoping this book can solve. And that's why you bought this, and it's the reason you're still reading it.

Your problem was that you want to get into email marketing but aren't sure where to start, and the solution is to give you the lowdown on how to get into it and master it. Once you understand what category the majority of your subscribers fall into, you can then start tailoring your content so that you can boost your sales.

But What If You Have Both?
If you have both types of subscribers, that's awesome. It's indeed the best thing. After all, what could really be better than a solution seeker who is also a fan? They love what you're all about, and you're solving their problem. Win!

In this event, your subscribers will probably buy literally everything you sell while promoting your product. They will also share a testimonial, too. These subscribers are incredibly good for business, and you need to look after them. Keep them on your good side and you'll go far. All it takes is a few raving customers to shout your name from the rooftops and you can strengthen your emailing marketing list even more.

And let's say that you have more fans than solution seekers, but want to turn your fans into solution seekers. How would you go about doing it?

You could start by asking your fans about their problems. What issues do they have that you can solve? You can do this on Facebook. Engage with your fans, find out what's missing from their lives and what you could be helping them out with.

If you're a member of Facebook groups, you've surely already seen the group leaders ask their fans what problems they could help them with. It's an easy way of turning fans into solution seekers. If you don't engage your fans in this way, they'll always remain your fans. But you won't be getting as much out of them as you could be doing. For years, they may have had a problem you could solve. But until you asked them about it, you'll both lose out.

Understanding Who Your Subscribers Are
If you decide to coast through email marketing without ever understanding your subscribers, you'll fail. That might sound harsh but it's true. You won't get anywhere unless you understand your customers.

It's what the success of any business hinges on. The more you know your customers, and the more you understand what problems, needs and wants they have, the more success you will have.

How do you find out more about your subscribers? There are a few ways:

• Phone calls
• Surveys
• Live events
• Social Media

You could also hang out in the kind of online forums where your target audience is likely to post stuff. You could join relevant Facebook groups and take note of the discussions that are taking place. What concerns do people have? What's missing from their lives that YOU could solve? It's only once you have such information about a customer (or once you have profiled them) that you can then use the info to create the kinds of services, tools and products that they actually want. As opposed to ones you think they want.

Remember, knowledge is power.

It's too easy to stay locked up in your ivory tower. But guess what? It's actually really easy, fun, and useful to get out among your customers. Once you do this, you can start adding value to your emails. You can start pricking their ears by giving them something they actually want. Invest time in getting to know your audience. It's worth it.

CHAPTER 3: HOW TO BUILD AN EMAIL LIST

At some stage, you will need to build an email list. In this chapter, you'll learn how to do this step-by-step.

First Step - Get Yourself An AutoResponder
You can download a free auto-responder, such as LaunchRock. LaunchRock is actually great, and super easy to set up and use. Its deliverability rates are good, and it offers a few attractive opt-in forms and squeeze page templates.

Templates are good because it's super important that your opt-in forms and squeeze pages look good. And if you design them yourself, chances are they won't look so great.

MailChimp is also free, and easily one of the most popular auto-responders. You've probably already seen its name in your inbox, as emails sent using MailChimp lets customers know they've been sent with MailChimp. However, despite its popularity, and despite what a lot of growth hackers might be telling you, MailChimp isn't so great. Its deliverability rates are alarmingly low, while its templates are worse than you could probably do yourself.

Alternatively, if your budget allows for it - get a paid auto-responder instead. And indeed there are a good number of high quality paid auto-responders out there. Moreover, they don't cost a massive amount of money, and you could easily find a good one for around $15 per month.

GetResponse is generally considered by email marketers to be one of the better low-budget ones available. They're considered reliable and hassle-free. It's also an affordable way of ensuring you grow a successful emailing list in the long-run.

Aweber is great too. They have some good-looking templates, as well as some funky, standout opt-in forms.

Second Step - Create Your Opt-In Form
The next thing you need to do as you build an email marketing list is create your opt-in form.

To quickly recap, an opt-in form is the form a customer fills in when they want to subscribe. Usually, they just fill in their email address and name, but some forms ask for a few more details, such as location and age.

You don't need to create your opt-in form out of thin air. Instead, your auto-responder will provide you with the tools to make a start. However, it's up to you to work on the design.

Any good auto-responder (including the free ones) will provide you with a custom design tool to help you get started. You can use this tool to alter the fonts, color, size and a few other features of the form so it corresponds with your branding better.

Creating a smart, visually appealing opt-in form isn't easy. If you're not a designer and don't have an eye for this sort of thing, get yourself over to a global freelancing platform such as Upwork.com and hire a freelance designer. It's worth it.

An important part of the opt-in form is the thank you page. When someone subscribes to your list, you should redirect them to a confirmation and thank you page. It's a great way to start a relationship with your potential customer and audience. It also helps reassure them that they made the right choice.

A generic thank-you page is something else that's taken care of by your auto-responder. You can either tweak this generic thank-you or leave it as it is. You can also create your own from scratch.

Again, if you have no experience with design, it's worth hiring a freelance designer to design a thank-you page for you. It's hardly going to fill a subscriber with excitement if they're redirected to a rather bland thank-you page is it?

You also need to create an already subscribed page link just in case someone signs up who's forgotten that they've already signed up. You'd think this wouldn't happen, but it does. Don't spend much time on creating this page. In fact, you can use your thank you page but just tweak the text.

Third Step - Creating A Web Page For Your Opt-In Form
You've got your opt-in form. Great. Now you need somewhere to host it. And you might not believe it but - yep - this is something else that your auto-responder can take care for you.

However, while an auto-responder can indeed host your web form on its own website, this isn't always the best idea if you want to maximize your conversions.

It is, however, free, and easy to set up. In fact, all it usually takes is just one click and voila! you're all done. It's perfect for anyone who doesn't know a lot about HTML or coding. And it's the option best recommended if you're a total beginner.

However, if your budget allows, it's best to look at paid options like LeadPages. This is an excellent service for landing pages and squeeze pages that convert well.

Another option you have is to include your opt-in form on your own website or blog if you already have one. However, you must have full control over your website. In other words, it must be self-hosted. Otherwise, you won't be able to do it.

Fourth Step - Do You Want A Single Opt-In Or Do You Want A Double Opt-In?
Some people choose to go with a double opt-in, in which case they need a second web page, otherwise known as a confirmation page. Basically, once they've subscribed, the second opt-in page asks them to confirm that their information is correct.

The second opt-in page can help to iron out any mistakes the customer has made, but if a customer was hesitant about signing up in the first place it could also give them a chance to change their mind. So it's a bit of a double-edged sword. It's up to you to decide if you need one.

Fifth Step: Creating A Deliverable Or A Gift
This fifth step is entirely optional - but it's highly recommend. Once someone has opted-into your email list, it's then down to you to make good on your promises to them. Let's say you promised them a free video if they signed up. If so, you then need to include this free video on the thank-you page.

Otherwise, they'll be wondering where the heck their free stuff is! And they might get grumpy. Make sure that they can access their free gift instantly. Why delay when your auto-responder can take care of it for you? Just link it to them on the thank you page and keep them happy. It's the wisest choice and customers love it.

Sixth Step - Setting Up Your Thank You Page
A thank you page should be pretty self-explanatory, but there is more to it than a simple "Thank You For Signing Up!"

On your thank you page, you can include - as just mentioned - a link to the free gift, as well as instructions for what the next steps are. What is the customer meant to do next? If you don't tell them on the thank you page, they won't have a clue regarding what they're supposed to do next!

Seventh Step - Writing Your AutoResponder Series
The next step to building your email marketing list involves writing your auto-responder series. The aim with this is to create a better, tighter relationship with your customers, while also educating them and offering them products they want to buy.

Your debut auto-responder email is your welcome email. It needs to include the link to the free gift you promised them (this is incase they didn't see it on the thank you page), and you could also include a taster of what's to come in future emails. Let them know what the score is, and what kind of content you'll be firing out.

Here is an example:

"Check your inbox for free tips, tricks and hacks, as well as my own personal story of how my eBook sales on Amazon Kindle shot up from zero to 10,000 in less than one month."

Whatever you tease them with in your welcome email has to be true. And you also need to make good on your promise. There is nothing worse than an email marketer creating these sky-high expectations before failing to deliver on them.

Eighth Step - Testing Your System

So far, so good. You've done the groundwork and got everything ready. You're ready to go! But calm down partner. There is still some work to do before you're at the finished line. Now it's time for testing.

Do what your subscribers have to do - sign up for your own emailing list! Sounds crazy? It isn't. The idea is that by completing all the steps your subscribers have to complete, you're seeing the opt-in process through their eyes. You're seeing what works, what doesn't, and you're also getting the chance to spot any glaring errors (such as really embarrassing spelling mistakes).

Testing your system lets you see that everything is working as it should be. Focus on this bit - you don't want to miss any glitches that your customers will spot, or will sabotaging the opt-in process to a point where a customer can't opt-in even if they wanted to. (Yes, broken opt-in forms do happen.)

It's also a good idea to test your web pages on different browsers to check how they look and what the upload speed is. It's a formality and it's boring, but it ensures your customers aren't met by any rubbish surprises along the way. Moreover, it will also ensure that your conversion rates don't plummet.

Here is a checklist for you:

1.) Test your web form
2.) Test your confirmation page
3.) Test your confirmation email
4.) Test your thank you page
5.) Test any links
6.) Test the already-subscribed page
7.) Test all of this on each browser, from Chrome to Safari

Ninth Step - Get Yourself Some Traffic
Unfortunately, subscribers don't just appear magically out of thin air. Nor do they automatically come to you. Instead, you need to find ways of directing them to your web page without phoning them up individually.

The hard work starts now, but driving traffic can be easier than some people make it out to be. For one thing, you should always, ALWAYS link to your squeeze page each time you upload fresh content. This is a trick that so many new marketers miss. It's simple and boosts conversions.

A link to your squeeze page should be everywhere. It should be included with your email signature, in each blog post, at the end of each video, as well as anywhere else you can think of. Essentially, the more you can link to your squeeze page, the greater the traffic you are driving. It's basic math, but in email marketing we call it "free traffic." Why? Because it costs no money at all! PPC advertising, on the other hand, is paid traffic as you pay for the clicks.

Is there a silver bullet when it comes to driving traffic to your squeeze page? Sadly not. What works for one person might not work for you and vice versa. Each online marketer you talk to will tell you that their method is the best, but that's not entirely true - it's the best method for them and their product. It doesn't mean it's going to help you build your own email marketing list.

So you should live by the saying that there is more than one way to bake a cake. Try different methods. Don't try one thing and settle. Experiment. Traffic is your bread and butter. You need it, so don't sell yourself short.

Tenth Step - Sending Out Broadcast Emails
What is a broadcast email? Put simply, it's just like any other regular email you send out to someone you know. The difference is that this time you're not sending it out to a buddy - you're sending it out to your emailing list instead.

There is a second difference, too: whereas you don't schedule the emails you fire off to a friend, you will probably be scheduling your broadcast emails. You don't have to, but it's a good idea to have a buffer by writing two or three emails at a time and then lining them up for the next few weeks.

These scheduled emails come in handy for whenever you've got something major to announce, such as a webinar, a discount or a promotion.

Eleventh Step - Start Using Conversion Tracking And Analytics

In the final step, you need to start using conversion tracking and analytics tools.

First, the big question that a lot of new email marketers ask: Do I really need analytics? Short answer – Yes You Do!

Without analytics, you'll be fumbling around in the dark. You'll be trying to find the hoop with a basketball after someone's blindfolded you and spun you around several times. Analytics may sound a bit complicated and scientific, but the long and short of it is that if you don't use analytics, you won't be a success at email marketing.

Analytics is the difference between an unprofitable business that's going no where and a profitable business that's soaring to the skies. That really is the difference. The success of your business hinges on analytics and it's important to understand this.

A few decades ago, they used to say that half the marketing budget was just going to waste. But no one knew which half. Why? Because they didn't have analytics at their disposal. But you do. So use it. Otherwise, you'll be at fault for wasting half your marketing budget when you could have avoided doing so.

With the right analytics tool properly implemented, you can see how successful your marketing campaign is. In other words, you can see whether or not your money is working for you. As such, you get the chance to close down unprofitable marketing campaigns before they really cost you, while scaling up the ones that are working.

Maybe you've watched on in envy as online entrepreneurs have gone from zero to hero super fast. One moment their business was doing nothing, and the next it was soaring. The reason? Analytics.

Analytics can help your business grow up to ten times faster than it is doing at the moment. The data it offers lets you make the right decisions. In other words, knowledge is power.

Lifetime Value of a Customer
Do you know what the lifetime value of your average customer is? With analytics, you can find out.

The Lifetime Value of a Customer (LVT) is how much a customer is going to bring to your business over the course of their lifetime. Let's say that you use analytics and now have a picture of your average customer. You know that each year for the next five years that your business is in business, the average customer spends $100 in your store. This means that their LVT is $500. Why do you need to know this information?

Good question. You need to know what your LVT is because you can then work out how much you can spend on attracting new customers while still turning a profit.

Essentially, you don't want to spend more on marketing than customers are spending in your store. If you do, you'll look pretty silly. But to avoid this from happening, you need to know what your LVT is. And this is just one of the things that analytics can help you with.

Google Analytics

Google Analytics is the most popular analytics tool in the world, and indeed when people tell you to use analytics they basically mean that you should use Google Analytics. It's free, easy to sign-up to, and easy to use.

It's really detailed and provides you with accurate analytics on your site visitors. You can find out page views, bounce rates, conversion rates and so on.

You don't even need to be familiar with coding to use it, although to get the most out of it you will need to do a bit of reading up about the tool first. For example, not everyone is aware that there is a certain piece of HTML that has to be placed on their web page before Google Analytics starts to track the page.

CHAPTER 4: THE POWER OF SQUEEZE PAGES TO ACCELERATE YOUR LIST

To quickly recap: Your squeeze page is where people are encouraged to opt-into your email list. Either they're going to opt-in, or they're going to exit the page.

And because you want them to opt-in, your squeeze page needs to be good. It is, after all, your chance to sweet-talk the customer into getting them to make the decision you want them to make.

A squeeze page is generally basic in terms of what is on there. It's not recommend to include an outbound link, nor any navigation bars. Doing so will just distract your visitors from the main goal, which is to subscribe. That's all you want them to do. So don't distract them with other links.

Your squeeze page is your workhorse when it comes to building your emailing list, as this is where - in theory - most of your conversions will happen (or should happen). If most of your conversions are happening elsewhere, your squeeze page isn't good enough. See, the squeeze page is where you clinch the deal, and it should have at least a 5x better conversion rate than a blog.

According to the stats, an opt-in box on a blog converts anywhere from 1 to 4%, whereas the squeeze page aims for between 10 and 40%. The numbers are there for all to see. So you should be making it your aim to drive traffic to your squeeze page and convert people from there.

Let's Build A Squeeze Page

LeadPages is great for building squeeze pages, as it's quick, efficient - and easy. Moreover, LeadPages lets you track your conversions instantly, and it also sets you up with a split test that lets you tweak and boost your results.

Using WordPress To Build A Squeeze Page For Free

There is always WordPress of course, and the great thing about WordPress is that it lets you use its plug-ins to create a squeeze page for free. If your budget is tight, it's probably a good idea to go with one of WordPress' free plug-ins to start with. If, however, you have more money, you should use LeadPages. It'll cost you around $250 a month, but will produce better results. And since you're focused on the long-term here, you'll eventually claw back any initial outlay you make at the moment.

CHAPTER 5: GETTING TRAFFIC AND BUILDING YOUR LIST

Do emailing lists build and create themselves? Some online marketing gurus might have told you they do. But they don't. Sorry to burst your bubble. You might have a vision of email marketers making lots of money while doing little work. Perhaps they always seem to be travelling to places and taking vacations. But remember - these are just snapshots of a persons life. They're not showing you all the hard work that's going on in the background.

And when you first start out in email marketing - when anyone first starts out in email marketing - there is a LOT of work to be done. It's not plain sailing at all. The hard work starts straight away. To do well in email marketing, you need to find ways of driving traffic to your website. Essentially, you need targeted traffic.

What's targeted traffic? Targeted traffic is traffic you WANT as opposed to traffic you don't want. Is there such a thing as traffic you don't want? Surely all traffic is good traffic? Nope!

Bad traffic is traffic from users who have stumbled on your page but who are never going to be your customers. They're random visitors who quickly realize they have no use for this page and beat a hasty retreat within a second. Targeted traffic is traffic that's coming from your customers. In other words, it's your target audience.

How To Turn You Contacts Into Subscribers
If you've got a few subscribers who you've been shooting a few emails to without resorting to an auto-responder just yet, add this list to your auto-responder. However, you can only add them if they've been asked to be added. Do not under any circumstances add anyone who hasn't requested that you add them. It could get you in a lot of trouble and damage your brand.

Blogging
Most email marketers will tell you that the easiest way to build your emailing list is by kicking off a blog. All you need to do is blog regularly, and include an opt-in form on there. Before you know it, you'll be getting new subscribers! It's not, of course, so simple as all that. The reality is that for every one-hundred site visitors, only one may opt-in.

Placing the opt-in form to the top right of the page works best when it comes to conversions. It has a possibility of churning out a 5% rate with the opt-in form up there - and 5% is very good. That's basically one out of every hundred visitors that's visiting the blog.

Video Marketing

You should start making the most of video marketing. Everyone else is doing it. Why? Because it works! Today's generation is visual. Granted, the idea of filming yourself can be a bit daunting. But if you can get over your initial concerns, you will find that posting video content onto YouTube is an excellent way of boosting your conversions.

Like most strategies, video marketing is a long-term strategy. It's also the one that comes out on top, outperforming all the rest.

What kind of video should you upload? Not a funny one. Not a cat one. Not even one that's advertising your services. Instead, you should upload a video that HELPS people. Just a short, five-minute educational video on a subject you know inside out can be all it takes to help build your list of subscribers. Educational videos are easier to find, too. For example, if your video is on copywriting tips, it might be titled something like "How To Become A Faster Writer."

If you do edit together a video, don't forget to include the link to the opt-in page. That's the most important bit - that's why you put yourself in front of the camera in the first place.

Now, YouTube isn't going to make your conversion rates soar through the roof. Generally, opt-in pages linked to your YouTube videos have conversion rates of up to 1% but as low as 0.1% depending on the number of years it's been on the platform. Now, that doesn't sound like a HUGE amount. But if you can get thousands and thousands of people watching your videos over five years, it's quite a lot.

So, the way you caption your video is important. In the description box, include the link to your squeeze page in the very first line.

Public Speaking
This is terrifying for many. Starting with making videos - which is hard enough - to you getting on-stage in front of a bunch of people and speaking to them can feel impossible. But it's something that you should learn to be comfortable with.

If you have the confidence to speak publicly about your products and/or services, there is no good reason why you shouldn't do it. You don't even need to be selling anything. You should instead be giving something away for free to those in the audience who sign up to your list.

It's all about getting subscribers. And if you don't mind public speaking and already do it often, now is the time to start letting your audience know that you've got a great list that they're missing out on. Otherwise, it's YOU that's missing out.

Media
Similarly, if you regularly do podcasts, radio or TV interviews, you need to start telling people all about your emailing list.

Don't, of course, just say "Hey! I've got a great emailing list you should sign up to." You need to give them a reason for signing up. In other words, you need to romance with them a free offer. If you're a regular on podcast or the radio, it's a good reason to mention your list. You've got a great platform, so use it.

Pay-Per-Click Ads
Per-per-click ads (PPC), are a great way of driving more traffic to your squeeze page. Google AdWords and Facebook Ads are two of the most popular pay-per-click ads platform, but Facebook Ads are

especially fantastic because their targeting is so advanced.

You can easily find users whose interests match your target customers' interests. And once you've managed to put them in front of your squeeze page, you've hit the jackpot. It's game, set and match.

Also, when you combine split tests with PPC and analytics, your profits could go through the roof. Seriously. Moreover, getting PPC ads right off the bat is difficult. Most people find it hard, and it takes them time to get into the swing of things. This costs money after all. LeadPages, however, can save you time, money and hassle. It's a split-testing system that lets you run numerous split tests so that your conversions improve.

It's not recommended that you start with a big budget. In fact, it's best you start with a small one, run a few split tests, and continue running them until you know which landing pages and ads make the most money for your business.

How much do these split-tests cost? Quite a lot - a few thousand dollars at least. To make your PPC ad campaigns profitable, you will also need to dedicate a fair amount of time to split-testing, too - up to twelve months, perhaps.

It sounds like a lot. However, these are "worst case scenarios." Some maverick marketers have managed to make their PPC ad campaigns popular while pumping in very little cash and carrying out very few split tests. With PPC ads, you will make mistakes. But the key - like it is with anything in business - is to fail fast and learn from your mistakes.

Email Signature
My final tip for driving more traffic to your squeeze page involves maximizing your email signature so that it becomes a workhorse for you.

If you don't already have an email signature, now is the time to get one. Included in your signature should be a link to your squeeze page, as well as a link to your landing page and blog. Put it all on there. This is an opportunity to turn your day-to-day emails into lead gen opportunities. And the best thing about it? It doesn't require any extra work from you!

CHAPTER 6: COMPOSING EMAILS FOR YOUR SUBSCRIBERS

Okay, this is it. This is where you entice your subscribers with your informative, engaging and entertaining emails that get them to take the action you want them to take. You already know about traffic and you understand conversion rates - now it's time to put the word out there and show them what you've got.

Let's start with the subject line.

Subject Lines
If your subject line is poor, your subscribers probably won't even open up your email. They may as well not have subscribed in the first place!

Your subject line has to be as good as your best pick-up line - every single time. If it isn't, you're going to keep missing the spot. You might have a list of subscribers as long as your arm, but they're all totally useless to you if they aren't opening your email. Convincing someone to opt-in is one thing. Convincing them to open up and read your emails is another. And until they start opening your emails, the relationship is going nowhere.

It's like dating sites. How hard is it to get someone to read your messages? Very hard. Your opening line has to be a killer. Otherwise, they're not going to waste their time.

According to research, a good subject line should be no more than 9 words. If it is, it's too long. People on the Internet have VERY short attention spans. If your subject line is long and meandering, no one is going to get to the end of it. You need to get people to read to the end of your subject line, and you must make sure it's a brief journey.

The Problem With Spam Filters
The problem email marketers face are spam filters. Now, spam filters are just doing their job. They're there to protect the user from rubbish, scammy, junk emails that questionable characters are dumping in their inbox.

Because there are so many nefarious characters on the Internet trying to make a quick, unethical buck out of unsuspecting Internet users, spam filters now ban certain words. If you don't want your emails to get flagged and re-routed to someone's spam folder, you need to avoid the following words in your subject lines:

- Clearance
- Buy
- Earn $
- Additional Income
- Bargain
- Make $
- Opportunity
- Affordable
- Sale
- Opt In
- Ad
- Open
- Click
- Million

Some of these are clearly ridiculous. Just because you're using a word like "opportunity" doesn't mean you've got some sort of devious, underhanded money making tactic on the go. But it's all about context, and these words are frequently used in spammy emails. So they're basically out.

Subject Lines And Split-Testing Emails
A lot of auto-responders (even the free ones) come with a split-testing function that lets you split test your email copy and subject lines.

If you do decide to go down the route of split-testing your emails, it's best to begin with subject lines. What does this mean? Basically, half the people in your list receive an email containing subject line 1, and the other half get an email containing subject line 2. As soon as the emails are out, you can check your data and analytics to see how well they're doing - ergo, which ones are being opened more.

If there is a noticeable difference between the two in terms of how successful they are, it tells you what subject lines to focus on and which ones to ditch. Without a split-test, you just wouldn't have this kind of knowledge. And once you do know which subject lines are killer, you can make a note of them in a file on your laptop so that you can refine and tweak them for future emails. This is what all the best marketers do.

Essentially, you're learning what your audience likes and what they don't like. It isn't rocket science, but so many would-be email marketers rush into email marketing and completely ignore basics like these.

Size Of Your Font
For whatever reason, the default font size on all the popular auto-responders is 12. Generally, you should ignore the default font size and balloon it to 14. Why?

Because it just looks more readable. Who is going to bother to read an email with small font?

Email Spacing For The Mobile
Something else that a lot of would-be email marketers ignore is the fact that so many emails are opened on mobile phones. In fact, most are. And you know what that means, right? Yep, it means a smaller screen. You've got to respond to this with emails whose width have been optimized so that they are viewable on mobile phone screens.

This is a common mistake a lot of newbie's make all the time - emails that are just too big. They're hard to read, and they look really unprofessional. Not cool. Aim for a pixel width anywhere from 320 to 500 pixels. No more and no less.

Developing Email Templates
The auto-responder you use should give you the option of creating a template. Set the template to 14 pt. size, and modify its width so that it's compatible with mobile screens. Do this and you don't have to keep creating new templates each time you write a new email.

Track Your Clicks

Auto-responders usually lets you choose whether or not you want to track clicks.

For some, they recommend disabling this feature but it's quite useful. If you don't track clicks, you simply won't know what's working and what isn't.

CHAPTER 7: LIST MANAGEMENT HACKS

A lot of people start to feel overwhelmed when they get into email marketing and their list starts to grow and grow. They thought they could manage it. After all, it's just a list, right? No big deal. But when these lists grow, they really can take on a life of their own and they can be tricky to manage.

As well as length, there are also other issues, which can easily beset your emailing list, such as backing it up in case it malfunctions, and you lose all your subscribers (it doesn't happen often, but it can happen.) In fact, this is a good place to start: **backing up your emailing list.** It's really important that you do this, especially if your emailing list gets really big.

Can you imagine losing all those contacts you've worked so damn hard to acquire? It's a bit of a nightmare scenario. As soon as your list gets to a point where you feel that this email marketing thing is really taking off and going places, it's time to invest a bit of cash into backing it up two times in the event of losing it all.

How can email marketing lists go missing? It sounds a bit strange to suggest that an email marketing list can go missing, and they rarely do. But if your auto-responder provider happens to go bankrupt or otherwise shuts down their business, you're left with nothing. Or, it might get hacked. It's also possible YOU might get hacked. Either scenario is scary.

Setbacks happen to all businesses, and it's the unexpected ones that hurt the most. And while you can't prevent your email marketing list from ever going missing, you can at least mitigate the consequences or survive them altogether by backing up your list. And don't just do it this one time today or tomorrow. Do it often. Do it once a month.

It's like when someone's editing a video and they keep saving their changes because they know that at any minute something could go wrong and they can easily lose all their work. The flaw with technology is that, as great as it is, things do go wrong with it.

How you go about securing your list by backing it up depends on the auto-responder you've been using. You can email their support team to find out how you'd go about it, or you could just Google how to do it with that specific auto-responder. The answer will be out there.

Once you've got the back-up list in its own file, you should then save it somewhere like DropBox, or any other cloud-based folder that's super secure and won't let you down.

Your List's Value

How do you determine your lists value? There is a checklist that helps:

• Your list is big
• You have a good relationship with those who subscribe
• You offer lots of services and products
• You have a good marketing funnel
• Your list is well-targeted
• Your list is full of people who have bought similar services or products from competitors in the past
• You send out emails regularly
• Plenty of your subscribers click on your emails

If most of the above applies to you and your list, you're winning and your list is really valuable. Look after it. Back it up. Keep going!

Naturally, you won't be at this stage just yet. But once your list is a few months old, check back to this chapter to see how valuable your list is. At first, your numbers may well be small, but don't be discouraged. This is a marathon, not a sprint. There is a long way to go.

Pruning Your List

Every now and then, your list requires cleaning. Why? Because there isn't really any point keeping old subscribers on there who never even receive your emails.

Of course, there will also be subscribers on your list who can open your emails, but who are choosing not to - and never have done. Should you delete these? No, there's no need. Just get rid of the ones whose email addresses either don't exist anymore, or whose spam filter isn't letting your emails get through.

Occasionally, you might delete an active subscriber by mistake. It sucks when this happens, but to reduce the risk that it might happen, contact your auto-responder support team and ask them to walk you though the deleting process.

What You Can Do With The List Of Unsubscribed Emails

The more people that sign up to your list, the more there will be those who unsubscribe. Sucks? Well, a little bit. But it's just part and parcel of our trade. Some will stick around forever, others won't. You will get some folk who unsubscribe – everyone does. Don't take it as a personal attack. It's just that they aren't finding the content very useful. But what do you do with all these unsubscribed emails?

As underhanded as it sounds - and as underhanded as it is - there are some people who choose to SELL people's emails.

While this may be an unethical practice, there are some people who don't find fault in it. What most people with integrity do is simply delete the list. Sure, there will be marketers who tell you that not selling these email addresses means you don't reap the profits that can come from selling leads. But your reputation is at stake here. What would you rather have? A good reputation or a quick buck?

Remember, whatever you do with the unsubscribed email list should already be clearly laid out in the privacy policy.

Privacy Policy
There will be a privacy policy you'll need to write up, which is a legal document or statement that outlines what you'll be doing with client or customers' data. And since you're putting together an emailing list, you'll definitely need to come up with a privacy policy, too. You can't ignore this one. However, YOU can't do

all this yourself. Instead, you'll need to get in touch with a specialist, such as an attorney.

To get started, you could do a Google search on the templates for privacy policies, before drafting your own. Once it's all done, upload it to your website, and make sure there is a link to it from your squeeze page(s). In fact, you need to link to it from any page where there is an opt-in form.

If you do decided to rent or sell email addresses to third parties (and some email marketers do this), you need to let people know in the privacy policy. It won't be popular, and it may indeed lose you some potential subscribers. But you can't hide the fact that you're going to sell their addresses.

CONCLUSION

Email marketing is a long-term process. It's not something you're going to get right away. It takes dedication, time, preparation, money, and lots and lots of hard work. But hard work pays. And if you're prepared to put in the hours, and spend time tweaking your methods and growing your list like a gardener grows their flowers, email marketing could be the best thing that's ever happened to your business.

You'll need to return to this book and other sources as you work on your list. Dip in and out of chapters for the information you need. Read other blogs on the subject, too.

Give the lessons and tips on here a shot and watch your email subscribers and business grow.

THANKS FOR READING

We really hope you enjoyed this book. If you found this material helpful feel free to share it with friends. You can also help others find it by leaving a review where you purchased the book. Your feedback will help us continue to write books you love.

The Smart Reads library is growing by the day! Make sure and check out the other wonderful books in our catalog. We would love to hear which books are your favorite.

Visit:
www.smartreads.co/freebooks
to receive Smart Reads books for FREE

Check us out on Instagram:
www.instagram.com/smart_readers
@smart_readers

Don't forget your 2 FREE audiobooks.
Use this link www.audibletrial.com/Travis to claim
your 2 FREE Books.

SMART READS ORIGINS

Smart Reads was born out of the desire to find the best information fast without having to wade through the sheer volume of fluff available online. Smart Reads combs through massive amounts of knowledge compiles the best into quick to read books on a variety of subjects.

We consider ourselves Smart Readers, not dummies. We know reading is smart. We're self taught. We like to learn a TON about a WIDE variety of topics. We have developed a love for books and we find intelligence attractive.

We found that each new topic we tried to learn about started with the challenge of finding the pieces of the puzzle that mattered most. It becomes a treasure hunt rather than an education.

Smart Reads wants to find the best of the best information for you. To condense it into a package that you can consume in an hour or less. So you can read more books about more topics in less time.

OUR MISSION

Smart Reads aims to accelerate the availability of useful information and will publish a high quality book on every major topic on amazon.

Smart Reads hopes to remove barriers to sharing by taking the copyright off everything we publish and donating it to the public domain. We hope other publishers and authors will follow our example.

Our goal is to donate $1,000,000 or more by 2020 to build over 2,000 schools by giving 5% of our net profit to Pencils of Promise.

We want to restore forests around the globe by planting a tree for every 10 physical books we sell and hope to plant over 100,000 trees by 2020.

Doesn't it feel good knowing that by educating yourself you are helping the world be a better place? We think so too...

Thanks for helping us help the world. You Smart Reader you...

Travis and the Smart Reads Team

WHY I STARTED SMART READS

Every time I wanted to learn about something new I'd have to buy 20 books on the topic and spend way too long sorting through them and reading them all until I arrived at the big picture. Until I had enough perspectives to know who was just guessing, who was uninformed and who had stumbled upon something remarkable.

I wished someone else could just go in and figure that out for me and tell me what matters. That's how smart reads was born. I want smart reads to be a company that does all that research up front. Sorts through all the content that is available on each topic and pulls out the most up to date complete understanding, then have people smarter than me package the best wisdom in an easy to understand way in the least amount of words possible.

For example, I got a new puppy so I wanted to learn about dog training. I bought 14 different books about dog training and by the time I got through the first 5 and finally started getting the big picture on the best way to train my puppy she had grown up into a dog.

Yeah she's well behaved. She doesn't poop in the house. I can get her to sit and come when I call. But what if someone else went in and read all those books for me, found the underlying themes and picked out the best information that would give me the big picture and get me right to the point. And I'd only have to read one book instead of 15.

That would be amazing. I would save time. And maybe my dog would be rolling over, cleaning up after my kids and doing the dishes by now. That my friend, is the reason I started smart reads. Because I wanted a company I can trust to deliver me the best information in an easy to understand way that I can digest in under an hour. Because dog training is one of many subjects I want to master.

The quicker I can learn a wide variety of topics the sooner that information can begin playing a role in shaping my future. And none of us knows how long that future will be. So why not do everything we can to make the best of it and consume a ton of knowledge. And I figured all the better if I can also make a positive difference in the world.

That's why we're also building schools, planting trees and challenging ideas about copyright's place in today's world. Because as a company we have to be doing everything we can to support the ecosystem that gives us all these beautiful places to read our books. Thanks for reading.

Travis

Customers Who Bought This Customers Who Bought This Book Also Bought

Passive Income: Do What You Want When You Want and Make Money While You Sleep

Understanding Affiliate Marketing: An Internet Marketing Guide for How To Make Money Online Using Products, Websites and Services

Blockchain Revolution: Understanding the Internet of Money

Unlocking Potential: Master the Laws of Leadership

The Everything Store Sales Guide: How to Make Money with Amazon FBA

A Detailed Guide in Building A Successful Photography Business Online: Learn How to Market, Sell, Promote and Make Money as a Photographer

A Simple Guide on How To Train Your Dog: Use Clicker Training to Teach Your Dog to Walk on a Leash, Sit, Stay, Go to Potty and Obey Your Commands

Mastering Your Time: Learn How Successful People Enhance Productivity, Beat Procrastination and Do More in Less Time